1993

Happy Christmas, Ryan

Love,
Mom + Dad

Quite a book......

Printed
For
Quixote Press
by
BRENNAN PRINTING
100 Main Street
Deep River, Iowa 52222
515-595-2000

IOWA'S OLD HOUSES
AND
NEW LOVES

by

Bruce Carlson

QUIXOTE PRESS
R.R. #4, Box 33B
Blvd. Station
Sioux City, Iowa 51109

i

© *1991 by A. Bruce Carlson*

* * * * * * * * * *

Although the author has exhaustively researched all sources to ensure the accuracy and completeness of the information contained in this book, he assumes no responsibility for errors, inaccuracies, ommisions, or any inconsistency herein. Any slights of people or organizations are unintentional. Readers should consult an attorney or accountant for specific applications to their individual publishing ventures.

QUIXOTE
PRESS
Bruce Carlson
R.R. #4, Box 33B
Blvd. Station
Sioux City, Iowa
51109

PRINTED
IN
U.S.A.

iii

DEDICATION

This book is dedicated to all the young lovers who knew Iowa when the summer winds moved through the prairie grasses.

The author wants to express his appreciation to the many people who have been of invaluable help by sharing family records. Without that help this book would be only a front and a back cover.

vi

TABLE OF CONTENTS

CHAPTERS

The reader must appreciate the fact that some of these stories could cause embarrassment to people living today. Because of that some of these stories use fictitious names. In these cases it should be understood that any similarity between these names and actual persons, living or dead is purely coincidental.

FOREWORD

Bruce Carlson has captured for us some accounts of romances associated with various of the old homes here in Iowa's Old House and New Loves.

Today as I drive past some of the homes he writes about, I have feelings about them that I wouldn't have known had I not read Iowa's Old Houses and New Loves.

I see all old houses in a different light now. What secrets do these early homes in Iowa know? What whispered words have been swept away by the wind and what rendezvous have been long since forgotten?

Prof. Phil Hey
Briar Cliff College
Sioux City, Ia.

PREFACE

As we drive along Iowa's highways and back roads, we pass countless early homesites.

Some of these are still occupied by families. Some are home only to some mice and maybe a coon or two. Some have the old house still standing, looking back at us with the vacant stare common to old houses that have lost their windows to the weather or an errant stone.

Still others of these old homesites can boast only a foundation or even just a row of trees than can no more than hint at what used to be.

Be they old houses still in use or long since silent, each has secrets about the people who have come and gone.

The passions of early Iowa loves lie cooled today behind the brick or wooden walls of these buildings, or under the green soil of the yard. But those folks were flesh and blood, and their loves were real. Many of us here today owe our very existence to these romances of years ago.

CHAPTER I

THAT DAVIS GIRL

lark Mann's resourcefulness was outweighed only by his shyness when he lived in Cedar Falls back in 1901.

Clark had seen the Davis girl there at the old Davis Mansion on occasion, but he had never worked up the courage to speak to her. It wasn't that he had always been that shy. He had, in fact, taken several of the other girls in town out to a picnic, a dance, or whatever. But it was different with Jane Davis. When he looked at her he lost all his courage, his recollection, and whatever reason he might have had.

Clark had seen Jane Davis on three different occasions; once while she was strolling out in front of the mansion and once downtown. The third time was when she was sitting on a park bench there in town. Each time that he saw her he could scarely believe that she could possibly be as beautiful as she was.

Jane had the classic fine and porcelain-white features so much in fashion back in 1901. Her voluminous skirts and petticoats were unable to hide the fact that she was, as they would say, "one fine figure of a woman."

All Clark knew about Jane was what little he was able to glean from what he hoped sounded like casual questions he asked of people who might have reason to know her. He had to be awfully secretive about his questions for fear that folks would notice his interest and accuse him of "putting on airs" by getting interested in the daughter of one of the fanciest families in town. One evening Clark went to an ice skating party just on the off chance that Jane might attend since he knew that a couple of her friends would be there. All he got for his trouble was cold feet and a good tongue lashing from a litte old man he mananged to knock over in a collision. It wasn't a very satisfactory situation.

Clark was pretty much resigned to the inescapable, but dismal conclusion that he would be able to admire Jane only from afar. He knew that she would have nothing to do with such a common person as himself when her family was so well-fixed and of such fine breeding. While he was rapidly falling in love with that unattainable angel, he refused to even let himself think in terms of that word. For he sensed that to do so would simply make that forbidden fruit all the sweeter.

Apparently Clark was inspired by the singing telegram idea because he did just that, or almost just that. He wrote a song that spoke movingly of a young lady's beauty and a young man's love for her. He practiced that song until he had it down perfectly.

Clark was amazed with himself that he had come up with such a good idea. All he had to do was to pretend he had been hired by a secret admirer to deliver the singing message.

Getting some clothes made that had the appearance of a uniform was the needed equipment for the ruse. That is, that was all he

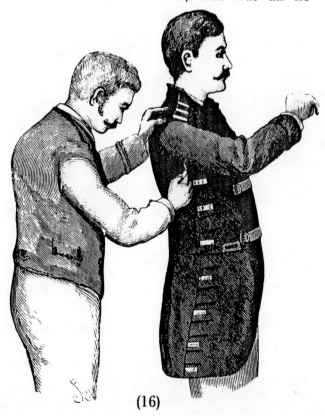

needed except for a photograph of a handsome young man. That was to be the photograph of a "secret admirer." He found that and was ready to put his scheme into practice.

Clark had watched the Davis place long enough that he pretty well knew Jane's schedule. On the big day he shaved and fixed himself up with great care. He wanted to look as good as he could when he met Jane, even if he would be pretending to be there for another person.

It was with a lot more than just a little bit of nervousness that Clark turned the ornate little knob on the crank bell of that fancy front door.

His heart was pounding so hard he could hardly hear the bell ringing there on the inside. Would she answer the door herself? If not, would she even  come to the door to hear the love song that he had so laboriously prepared for her?

Clark, by this time, almost wished that he hadn't

turned that knob, but it was too late now. He had set the whole thing in motion and couldn't back out at this point.

Since Clark hadn't heard any footsteps, he was surprised to see the knob turning. The shadow on the other side of the frosted glass told him that it was an adult male opening the door for him. He was right, for soon a distinguished looking man was looking at him questioningly.

"Hello, Sir. A singing message for Miss Davis, please."

Without a word, the man disappeared. Clark wasn't sure if he should stand there on the porch, step inside, or just leave.

Within a couple of minutes, however, Jane Davis appeared.

"A singing message?" she asked.

That simple question went unanswered for a few seconds as Clark fought to get his breath coming again. He was so taken with Jane's beauty he could hardly function. He had never seen her up this close before, and wondered how she could be so beautiful. In those few moments he found himself thrilled that he had come up with this really great idea.

"Yes, Madam, I've been hired to deliver this message to you by a gentleman who would not divulge his name. He did, however, ask me to give this to you."

With that Clark handed that lovely young lady the photograph of the "secret admirer."

As Jane proceeded to extract the photograph from its case, Clark started to sing. He was so impressed by Jane he knew he had to get started or he would be unable to do it if he waited any longer. There she was, only four or five feet away, looking all in the world like she was some sort of heavenly blossom that the angels had dropped here onto Earth from on high.

Jane looked questioningly at the photo while Clark

sang. The fact that those words had, unknown to Jane, come directly from his heart, made them all the more meaningful to him. The genuineness of those lines must have made an impression on her. Clark could tell that she was really moved. She studied the photograph carefully, obviously trying to fathom who that secret admirer could be.

"Is the photograph mine to keep?" she asked as Clark concluded his song.

"Yes, Madam. The gentleman so instructed me," as he tipped his "uniform's" hat.

"You have no idea of the name of this fellow? Is that right?"

"That's right, Madam. I'm just delivering the message."

"Well, I declare. It certainly is a nice song. Thank you very much."

The memory of those few minutes saw Clark through the next several days after his brash little trick.

He hadn't really planned, orginally, to do it more than once, but decided that would be a good way to see the lovely young lady yet once again.

So, once more, he went to that ornate door and summoned the same man. Again, that fellow disappeared into the house without a word. In a couple of minutes Jane came to the door as she had the previous time.

Clark had worked quite a while on that second song and was sure that it would be well received.

This time when Jane came to the door she had a smile on her lips and immediately opened the door wider as if to invite Clark in.

Clark could tell that Jane enjoyed the novelty of the situation. She smiled and laughed delightfully a couple of times during the song.

When Clark was done Jane motioned to a dish of mints as if to invite him to have some and asked him to wait a moment. With that she disappeared up the ornate stairway into the hall above. When she returned a couple of minutes later, she had that photo that Clark had given her on his first visit.

"Would you ask your employer to sign this for me?"

Clark was more than happy to comply, for that would offer a reason for him to come back yet another time.

"Yes, Madam. I shall be glad to."

Clark's joyfullness over having a reason to return was tempered somewhat by his realization that the photograph meant enough to her that she would want it signed. It was, after all, the photo of another person. While he was in no position to feel any jealousy, he nevertheless, did know the ache of envy.

Clark loved Jane dearly, and there she was, being interested in the photo of another. The fact that this other person was Clark's own invention did little to comfort him.

Clark labored long that evening to perfect just the right handwriting to impress Jane. After he thought he had it down well he wrote "From a Secret Admirer" boldly across the bottom of the photo.

Returning the photograph was simply the next of a number of times that Clark returned to the Davis mansion, each time with a different song from that secret admirer.

Each time he was there he grew to love Jane more, but he begin to feel the emptiness from being only a messenger. He longed to tell her of how he felt, but he knew that the moment he would do that, he would find that door slammed in his face. In 1901 in Cedar Falls a common person such as himself didn't presume to fall in love with such a high-bred person as Jane Davis. Cupid's arrows tended not to cross social lines back then.

It was during one of those times when he was thinking how he could hardly stand being so close to Jane when she surprised him.

"Please come into the parlor and tell me what you know of this man who is so persistant, and yet so secretive."

It was, of course, almost indescribably wonderful

to be able to sit and visit with Jane for a few minutes. Clark disclaimed any further knowledge beyond what he had told her, but it was wonderful just to be there. He toyed with the idea of revealing just enough to encourage her questions, for that would offer a reason to stay longer. He thought better of it, however, for fear of revealing that the whole thing was a hoax.

Three more times in a row Jane urged Clark to stay for a few minutes in the parlor to talk about that secret admirer.

Meanwhile, Clark's agony over not being able to reveal his own feelings grew even more of a burden to bear. It hurt him to no end to pretend to feel nothing, to be nothing beyond a messenger.

It was painful for Clark to hear Jane speak of matters of the heart, yet speak not of him.

As Clark's dilemma grew ever more burdensome, he finally decided he must end this self-inflicted pain. The only way to do that and to live with the situation, was to make a clean breast of it. He'd go that very evening and sing the one remaining song he had composed. His eyes would drink but

once more of her beauty before he walked out of her life forever. It was almost with a sense of relief that Clark made his decision. He would no longer be burdened with the need to see her without being able to reveal how much he loved her.

Jane was, somehow, even more beautiful that evening when he entered that now-familiar parlor. Smiling, she sat and motioned for Clark to begin.

It was fortunate that Clark had those verses well memorized for he was hardly able to sing the words. She was to beautiful there on the chair. He loved her so much!

The last line of the song almost didn't get sung because emotion filled his heart to overflowing.

"Miss Jane, I have something to say to you. It's important that I say these words, then I'll be gone."

Jane was taken aback a bit by that. Clark hadn't spoken to her in that way before.

"What is it? Do you have word from your employer?"

That question was more than Clark could bear. At

this crucial moment her mentioning him cut into Clark like a knife.

"No." he answered.

Clark's agitation and extreme discomfort apparently was contagious for Jane quickly rose to her feet as if words were trying to escape her lips.

"What I need to tell you" he said " . . . . . .is that this will be the last time . . . . . . "

"Wait, Don't say anything. I need to tell you something. And I can no longer pretend. I feel like an imposter. I no longer want to pretend an interest in your employer, whoever he is. I've been most unfair!"

"Unfair?" he asked, not understanding at all.

"Yes, unfair. He is wasting his time sending you with those beautiful songs. I love a man other than he. I love you."

CHAPTER II

THE THREE YEAR SECRET

he story of Frank Aven and Beth Frane is one that comes to us from their granddaughter, Mrs. Gayle Rassmussen of Topeka, Kansas.

It's a story that goes back to Council Bluffs in 1886 when Beth was a girl of only sixteen, living in what is now a broken down old house hardly capable of doing a decent job of providing refuge for the sparrows that fly in out of the shell that remains.

But, back in 1886 when Beth and her parents moved into the home, it was as nice a house as any
in the neighborhood.

Mr. Frane was a farmer, working not only their
own place, but also that of a neighbor's. All that
responsibility kept him awfully busy, but not too
busy to keep him from being so strict with Beth
that his behavior bordered on oppression.

Trips to town for farm folks have always been
something of a joyful occassion, but they sure
weren't for Beth. These trips were difficult for her
because of Mr. Frane's suspicious nature. Those
few moments when he wasn't watching Beth led
him to grill her mercilessly about where she went,
who she talked to, and asking if any boys talked
to her. He had to know exactly what she did every
minute.

Mr. Frane couldn't be everywhere at once, however, and one day while on the way home from church he found it necessary to leave Beth with the buggy while he walked home for a new wheel. Apparently his buggy wheel broke and broke badly enough that the buggy was totally immobilized.

Beth couldn't go with her father to get that new wheel for fear of ruining her Sunday clothes in the quagmire that passed for a road between Council Bluffs and Missouri Valley.

No sooner was Mr. Frane out of sight around the bend before young Frank Aven from Crescent came by on his way into Council Bluffs.

Now Frank didn't do just everything right, but he sure wasn't fool enough to pass by the Frane buggy without stopping. His excuse was, of course, to inquire if that lovely young lady sitting there needed any help.

"No, thank you. My father will be along very shortly."

Frank apparently wasn't going to be gotten rid of that easily, however, for he stayed and chatted with Beth for almost an hour. He had seen beautiful young ladies before, but he had never seen one that took his breath away like his new acquaintance there along the road.

Beth wouldn't have admitted it at the time, but she was really impressed with her visitor. He seemed to be so much nicer than the few neighbor boys she knew, a real gentleman in spite of his country looks.

During the course of their visit, Frank revealed that he was the new clerk at the dry goods store in Council Bluffs, having just come to the area from Harlan.

In their light banter back and forth, Frank extracted a promise from Beth that the next time she came to town and needed anything from their store, that she would buy it from him.

(32)

The look on Beth's face when she saw her father far down the road coming back with another wheel alerted Frank to the fact that he might not be a welcome sight to Mr. Frane. So, well before her father got to the buggy, Beth's new friend announced his need to be going, and then promptly left.

Beth knew she would face a lot of questions in the next few minutes when her father would want to know who that was that had stopped, and what they wanted.

She was right. In fact, he was already asking such questions before he got completely back to the buggy.

"Who was that, Beth?"

Beth wasn't accustomed to lying to her father, or

(33)

even having occasion to, so she surprised herself when she found her voice saying:

"Oh, it was a fancied-up couple from Omaha who wanted to know if I needed any help. We visited a while and then they left."

"What'd they say? Wuz there any boys with 'em?"

"No, Father, it was just this duded up couple that wanted to know if I needed any help. They were very nice."

Mr. Frane's suspicious eying of the "couple's" buggy, now well down the road momentarily made Beth wonder if he would try to check on her story by catching up with the buggy. She wasn't sure of how to do this lying and wasn't confident that she was very convincing.

Apparently, however, Beth's story rang true enough, for that was the last mentioned of the incident.

That wasn't all that was thought about it, however. Beth found that the attentions of that good-looking young fellow were nice. Even if he was kind of a rough-cut and homespun type, it felt good that he should be so interested in her.

So it didn't take Beth Long to come up with an excuse to go into that dry goods store a couple of days later when the Frane family went to town. She had suddenly "remembered" the need for some thread of a certain color when her mother was in the grocery store and Mr. Frane had an appointment to be at the hardware store for some bolts.

Beth had but a few minutes so she hurried to the store. She both hoped that her new friend would be there, and hoped he wouldn't. He was. She then almost hoped he wouldn't recognize her, but he did.

That brief encounter was but the first of several that were to follow in the next few weeks. Somewhere along the way, Beth and Frank fell in

love. He was eighteen and she was sixteen, and both dispaired that they would ever get to spend anytime together other than those few stolen moments in the dry goods store discussing the various attributes of fabric in loud voices, and their love in whispers. Both lived for those magic moments when they could allow their hands to touch or a shoulder to brush the other's.

Opportunities come in strange ways, however.

Apparently, along about the middle of April, Mr. Frane's hired man announced his intention to leave the first of May.

This, of course, posed a real problem for Beth's father who certainly didn't need to be without a hired man just when farming was getting into full gear.

With a flash of inspiration, Beth remembered that Frank had said one day that he was toying with the idea of hiring out as a hired man to a farmer. She could hardly wait to tell him of her father's need for a hired man there on the farm.

The day after his man made that announcement, Mr. Frane told his wife and daughter of his need to go to town.

"If you ladies need anything, you best be coming along. I'll be hunting a new hired man, and won't have time to be running any errands for you. I can't afford to not have any help around here."

"Well, yes, Father, I do need a couple of things at the dry goods store, so I'll come along."

Within a few minutes Beth and her father were pulling out of the yard on their way.

Mr. Frane's preoccupation with the need to find a new man probably distracted him from the fact that his daughter was awfully anxious to be on her way to the dry goods store.

As soon as Beth whispered to Frank the situation with the hired man, he recognized the possibilities. It wasn't but a few minutes later that Frank "accidently" met Mr. Frane over by the firehouse and allowed as to how he had heard talk about Mr. Frane needing a hired man.

Several questions and answers later, it was all but agreed that Frank could come to work for the Franes.

Frank was all ready with some convenient answers about what he had been doing recently. He wasn't going to reveal that he had been clerking at the dry goods store unless he had to. He thought that Mr. Frane might put two and two together, and come up with the realization that the whole thing had been set up.

The issue of having a fine young good-looking fellow for a hired man when he had that daughter around occured to Mr. Frane pretty quickly. When grilled about his attitude about girls, Frank explained that he had a girl friend over home and he sure wasn't interested in any of the local girls.

That set pretty well with Mr. Frane, and Frank was hired right there on the spot.

Within a few days Frank was living in the hired man's lean-to and having his meals with the Frane

family. When he was introduced to Mrs. Frane and Beth, he pretended that she was not more than just another farm girl he could care less about.

Over the next two years, Frank and Beth successfully hid the fact that they were in love. They covered up their relationship with the pretense of being slightly impatient with each other; nothing serious, just a mild case of antagonism that did a good job of hiding the reality of things.

Frank made a rather elaborate pretense of carrying on a faithful corrospondence with his girl back home. He would laboriously compose those "letters" of an evening. He would often ask Mrs. Frane how to spell a difficult word

in order that all should know about his letter

writing. On a couple of occasions Frank would ask Beth how to spell an word of endearment. She didn't think that was all that funny.

When Frank accumluated enough to start his own farm, he and Beth suddenly "fell in love." So Frank wrote his last letter to "the girl back home" and proposed marriage to Beth.

Frank and Beth were married in the spring of 1889 and their first child was born in 1890.

In the summer of 1906 when their son was sixteen, Beth and Frank told Beth's now aging father about the trick his daughter had pulled when she was sixteen. Mr. Frane didn't see the humor in it.

What thoughts passed between those two,
    as they spoke of thread and needle?

What words were thought, but went unsaid,
    those days so long ago?

How is a love kept secret,
    from the eyes of those around?

From what are made such strands
    to hold their words within?

We can only wonder at how it was,
    all those years ago.

When love was hid
    and an embrace was only a touch?

CHAPTER III

A PROMISE TO KEEP

e are all the products of the lives we've led before. Few of us have escaped unscathed from the acts of that person we were as children. All of us must pay for the errors we made so long ago when we were virtually different people than we are today.

So it was with Carole Dowling in the early years of the 1900s when she found herself a prisoner of a beautiful home south of Spencer. The chains that bound her were of her own making and were forged when she was just a teen-aged girl in 1896.

Carole Dowling, the adult, was an entirely different

person than Carole, the starry-eyed girl in 1896. For almost forty years, however, Mrs. Dowling suffered from an earilier girlish indiscretion.

It was in '96 when Carole was engaged to Christopher Dowling and the couple were talking about the sort of house they would buy or build upon their marriage the following year. Carole came from a family of modest means and would have been content with almost any sort of house had she thought enough about it to get her priorities squared around.

Carole, however, got kind of carried away with the excitement of the house issue. A problem was that Christopher's resources were sufficient that almost anything with in reason was possible. She could have, if she wanted it, just about the nicest house and furnishings that she could think of.

Only when something is possible, of course, are we burdened with the opportunity to make decisions about it. Suddenly little Carole found herself with the chance to make some big decisions about her future home.

This situation was so unique to this girl who had had so little to do with that she sort of went off the deep end. She truly loved Christopher and

would have loved him had he been as poor as she. In a moment of weakness Carole blurted out to her husband-to-be that since she could pick out any kind of house at all that she wanted, she would never never ask anything else of him.

Only half seriously did Christopher tease her by saying that he was going to hold her to that. While teasing her he made her repeat her vow, and extracted, from her, a solemn promise that she would stand by those words. He got her to promise that she would never never desert him, and that she would stay in the house he got for her come what may, through any circumstance, even with or without him. Apparently those words were born of a young lover's natural fear of losing the object of his adoration.

Since Carole loved him as much as he loved her, she found those promises easy to make.

I think we can assume that the "with or without him" part must have referred to the eventuality of Christopher dying early and leaving Carole the decision as to what to do about the house. Unfortunately, though, those fateful words "with or without him" came to have a different meaning shortly after the pair were married and had moved

into the house of Carole's dreams. Christopher's commitment to their marriage waned and then just disappeared altogether. The call of business led Christopher to spend more and more of his days away from home. It then became only a matter of time until Christopher dropped all pretense of having a happy home, and left his wife and house altogether. In short, he simply deserted her.

While Christopher's commitment evaporated, Carole's didn't. She had told him that she would stay there in that house come what may, and she was going to do what she had promised him.

That beautiful home soon became only a prison for Carole who grew to dislike the house. Her feelings about it didn't release her from her promise, however, for she stayed. The coming of the nineteenth century soon after Christopher left proved to be no cause for joy for Carole. All that seemed to tell her was that she had years and years of time to keep the promise she ached to be able to snatch back somehow.

But Carole wasn't the first person in the world to have said words she would have liked to take back. The promise still bound her to the house she soon learned to hate with the same passion that she once had known in loving it.

World War I came and went, as did the Roaring Twenties, and still Carole Dowling stayed on in that house. Her daily needs were tended to with money that Christopher had left when he left his bride. Her emotional and mental needs were met by the knowledge that she was keeping a promise. She was keeping that foolish vow she had made years earlier.

The coming and the ending of the Depression was akin to the coming and going of a new movie at

the theater in downtown Spencer where Carole never went. It didn't really touch her life at all. She was quite resigned to pass her time watching the birds in the yard outside her window.

Carole's assets weren't lavish, but were sufficient to see to her needs and the maintence of her hated enemy, the house she occupied.

No one in the community really knew what happened in the fall of 1935 when the Dowling house was suddenly abuzz with people. For several days the drive was filled with out-of-town cars. The windows that usually showed no lights were bright with lights burning every evening.

Then, after almost a full week of all that, Carole told her twice-a-week housekeeper and the gardner that their services would no longer be needed since she was moving away. Within twenty-four hours the house was empty, boarded up and obviously meant to be left unoccupied. That was the last that was seen of Carole Dowling. Within a few days the house was reduced to ashes in a fire and the land eventually went to the County for non-payment of taxes.

Lots of speculation proved to be only that; speculation. No one knew what became of Carole Dowling, or where she went.

Did she keep that promise for almost fourty years

only to finally break it? Was the fire an accident, or not? We know no more in 1991 than the folks did back in 1935.

Prison bars can be of iron,
   or stronger ones of words.

We spin the cords that bind us tight,
   as no one else can do.

And each of us must free ourselves
   of what we used to be.

CHAPTER IV

THE GHOSTLY CUPID

'm not sure if this is a love story, a ghost story, or simply an account of how Paula Hopkins pulled a fast one on Adam Hardin back in 1893.

Whatever kind of story it is, Paula and Adam did fall in love when Adam owned and lived in the old Hardin place down along the Skunk River southeast of Ames.

The whole thing started when Paula and Adam met at a church social in Huxley.

Paula had gone to that social somewhat reluctantly with a friend and was finally persuaded to go only because there didn't seem to be anything better to do that day.

Adam's reason for going was a bit more practical. He was a bachelor who quickly tired of his own cooking and welcomed a chance for some good old home cooking done by someone other than himself.

This pair ended up sitting across from each other

at a table on that beautiful late June afternoon there in the church yard.

From that point on, it was a whole new world for both Paula and Adam. Within a couple of weeks neither of them could figure out how they had possibly been able to get along without each other before. They were in love. They were so much in love they could hardly stand it.

Paula's heretofore carefully scheduled and organized life was suddenly turned upside down by this new experience. Adam would take her here and take her there. They went on innumerable drives, hikes, and outings of one kind or another. They went on horseback, by boat on the Skunk River, or by buggy. Adam's life on the farm got awfully busy as he tried to do all those farm chores and still carry on all that courtin'. If it came down to having to make a choice between some farm chore and the courtin', it was the courtin' that always won out.

It was obvious to everyone who knew the couple that it would just be a matter of time before Paula and Adam would be taking that fateful stroll down the aisle in that same church where the couple had met.

(55)

While it was obvious to everyone else, it sure wasn't to either Paula or Adam. It just never had occurred to Adam, and Paula began to dispair of his ever proposing. No amount of hinting on her part seemed to do the trick.

It was an ideal relationship other than that little problem with the lack of a proposal of marriage. The couple got along just handsomely and thrilled to the presence of each other as only lovers can do. On occasion Paula would descend on Adam's kitchen like a domestic whirlwind and shape up that pretty casually run place. She'd get it all shaped up and then prepare Adam a delicious supper. That little stratagy served to let Adam know how good a cook she was. From Adam's perspective, that was alright and freed up his time a bit to take Paula out driving more than he could have if he had to do all that cookin'. It also provided him some relief from a diet limited to the few recipes he knew. All in all, it was a good arrangement.

On those occasions when Paula would exercise her little show of domestic skills, she would liberally toss around hints about marriage. They didn't seem to take.

Paula learned early in her relationship with Adam an interesting thing about her boyfriend. The usefullness of that didn't occur to her for several weeks, however.

All of us have occasions now and then when a noise in the darkness will give us a start. We've all wondered, sometimes, just what that creak or groan on the stairs was. With Adam, it was considerably more than that. He was just plain scared stiff of ghosts and he didn't care who knew it.

Adam wasn't sure if he had ever actually seen a ghost or not, but that didn't make any difference. He was still scared of 'em. He would burn a  kerosene lantern all night there in his bedroom for what little security that light would offer. He had laid awake, wide eyed and listening, enough nights that he knew just about every creak and crack that the old house was prone to utter as it would settle, at night, into slumber.

It was one day when Paula and Adam were playing cards when he was telling about having heard a slight variation in the nighttime noises of his house that previous evening. His wide-eyed face and nervous voice revealed to Paula just how frightened he must have been that night.

That was the evening, as they played cards, that Paula came up with her idea. It was an idea that just might move Adam off of dead center and get him to propose.

Back in 1893 the water pail sitting there on the kitchen table was as common as the chairs around that table, or the wooden match dispensor over by the big old black cookstove.

Virtually every one of those buckets of water would also hold a long handled dipper that the folks would use to ladle water out into a pot or the sink. It was also common practice for family members to all drink directly out of that dipper.

Like most folks Adam was in the practice of "fetching up" a pail of water from the spring in the evening and setting it on the table so he'd have a nice fresh bucket of water come morning. A lot of the thrill of carrying water up from the spring

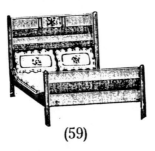

(59)

would seem to sort of get lost early in the morning when a guy first got out of bed and had sort of gotten used to the warmth of that bed while the ground outside would be wet or cold.

Adam was in the habit of taking a good drink from that dipper just before going to bed. It was that little habit that enabled Paula to pull that little trick on her boyfriend.

The first thing she did was to tell Adam that she had heard some stories about "The Scraping Ghost" that was showing up over around Ankeny. She told of how that "Scraping Ghost" would settle into a house and stay for weeks or even months.

"Why, they say it stayed in the Russel house for over a full year, they do. They claim that it hit Mrs. Russel with a heavy coffee pot while she was sittin' mindin' her own business one day."

"But, why do they call it the "Scraping Ghost?" Adam asked.

"It's 'cause they say it sounds like a piece of metal scraping on another one, kind of slow like, but just like tin or something. Isn't that odd?"

"Yeah, it's odd alright."

Adam was both bothered and fascinated by her telling about that ghost. He both hated to hear it, yet couldn't help but listen as Paula threw in some more details about how the ghost would almost always move into a house where a person would be living alone.

"In fact, over by Bondurant they don't call it "The Scraping Ghost". They call it the Widow's ghost 'cause it's like as not to move into a house where a widow or widower will live all alone. Widow Landis even saw the ghost playing the violin one night."

At this point Paula watched Adam closely, fearing that she might have pushed the point too far. It appeared that she had a good thing going, and she didn't want Adam to realize that he was being scammed.

"Alone, you say?"

"Yes, that's what they say."

Paula let all that soak in while she proceeded on with the second phase of her plan.

That second phase consisted of her getting into Adam's kitchen on the pretense of fixing him another nice supper. He was, of course, more than happy for her to do that again.

Paula chased Adam out of the kitchen while she prepared that meal. She sure didn't need him around while she sabotaged his water pail dipper.

Paula's next move was to very carefully push the bottom on that dipper in and out repeatedly, working on that dipper until all that crunching back and forth just pushed the metal too far and it developed a tiny crack. Paula could just barely see that crack when she looked as closely as she could right there where she knew it to be. She knew that he would never see it and would never know it was there. The water would leak so very slowly through that crack that he'd never suspect his dipper was anything but in fine shape.

Paula knew that Adam was in the habit of setting that long-handled dipper in the pail so it would float up on top of the water. She reasoned that the crack would slowly let the water in and eventually let it fill the dipper. She knew that the dipper would then slowly slide down the inside of the pail until it hit the bottom. She did enough experimenting with that pail and dipper to know it would make a really odd scraping sound as it slid down the inside of that water filled tin pail. It would get to vibrating as it slid down the side of the pail that made a real weird sound. She found that it would let the water in slowly enough that it would take about three hours after it was laid on top of the water for it to sink and make that noise. Then it would take almost half a minute for that dipper to scrap its way down to the bottom of the pail.

Now she was ready for the final phase of her plan. She waited a couple of days and then found occasion to talk about "The Widow Ghost" again. Once more, Adam was a reluctant, but fascinated audience as she spun one cold-blooded tale of terror about that ghost after another.

It was the third day after she rigged up that dipper when the ghost struck for the first time. Adam had been reading and then had gone to bed after taking his nightly drink from the water pail. As was his habit, he left the dipper floating on the top of the water in that pail, and walked away from it.

It was just about midnight when Adam awoke to one of the oddest and scariest sounds he had ever heard. He didn't realize at all that it was simply his dipper scraping down the inside of the water bucket as it sunk. All he heard was an erie sound of metal scrapping against metal. It was exactly the same sound that Paula had told about.

With a burst of energy born of stark fear; Adam sat up in bed. It was The Scraping Ghost! That ghost had come to his house!

Without waiting even a moment, Adam leaped out of bed and lit every lamp in the house in an effort to illuminate even the darkest corners.

Needless to say, Adam got no sleep the rest of the night and met Paula the next day, pretty much wrung out. Paula saw that and asked him what the problem was.

"Paula, I'm afraid The Scraping Ghost has come to my house."

"What do you mean, Adam?" she asked, knowing full well what had prompted that, and that she was the cause of it all.

Adam's story told Paula that things were working out exactly as she had anticipated. She lost no time in dropping some pointed hints about how The Widow's Ghost was always said to visit only those homes occupied by only one person. She'd follow that up with another hint about marriage.

A couple more visits by that ghost and a few more hints from Paula was all it took for Adam to come up with a brand new idea; that of marriage.

"Why, yes, Adam. I'll marry you."

"Well, let's go ahead and do it. We might as well do so right away, don't you think?"

Paula smiled a bit as she agreed that that would be alright.

Adam seemed almost indecent in his haste to tie the knot, and Paula wasn't about to let this opportunity slip from her grasp, so the pair were married within two weeks after Paula accepted.

Paula's first little chore in her new home was so common and unimportant that Adam didn't really even notice that she had purchased a new dipper to replace the rusted one he had had so long.

V

MOLLIE'S WAY

he road to romance, as we all know, can take some surprising twists and turns. That was as true in 1897 as it is today, in 1991.

And that was certainly true at the Hulpman house west of Davenport back then. In 1897 the Hulpman house was owned and occupied by a young businessman who had enough money to indulge in some modest luxuries.

That house was, of course, much more than James Hulpman needed for just himself, but it was available and already furnished with nice things. James admired that place a lot so he bought it.

James Hulpman had inherlted not only a rather impressive British lineage, but also enough resources to enable him to do such things. This young man was considered, of course, to be something of a prime catch by the young ladies of the community, but he wasn't interested.

James had been corresponding by mail with a girl back in England and was convinced that Anne was just the girl for him. He had never met her, but felt he all but knew her through those many letters the pair had exchanged. Apparently the two had started this correspondence through the urging of a mutual friend, and had written to each other for some time.

At age twenty-five, James decided it was about time he considered settling down. His dream was that it should be with Anne. He couldn't afford to take the time away from his school equipment business so he convinced Anne that she should come to America. He eagerly offered to pay the cost of passage if she would come to visit for a few weeks. Anne accepted. After

all, it simply would not do for them to start making any long-range plans until they had met.

Getting Anne to America also meant getting her servant girl, two little dogs and countless bags and trunks here also. It simply wouldn't do for a proper British girl to go traipsing off to America without a chaperone. She couldn't be parted from her pets, and the few things she planned to bring along were all absolutely necessary for those few weeks here on the edge of civilization.

While the subject of marriage had never been mentioned in so many words, it was generally understood by both James and Anne that that was a very distinct possibility. They knew, however, that they would have to go through the motions of meeting and falling in love, in person, so to speak.

As far as James was concerned, he had already done the latter, it was just a matter of meeting Anne to make it all official.

Anne, too, was predisposed to the idea of marriage with James. She had grown very fond of that brash young American with whom she had traded so many letters.

James had a full time man servant, and a part time gardener, as well as a part time housekeeper, so the Hulpman home wasn't exactly what you would call your typical bachelor pad. It was a well kept home, and certainly one of the nicest ones in the community.

For Anne's coming, however, nothing could be out of place. James needed to make an excellent impression on her, so he got a crew of men in for several weeks to redo the garden, completely paint the interior of the house, and otherwise shape up the area. A room was prepared for Anne's servant girl and the one for Anne was completely redone, all the way from painting the ceiling to installing a new rug on the floor.

It wasn't every day that a fancy young English-woman came to visit and James was going to do things up right.

After what seemed like an eternity to James, Anne finally arrived. The spring wagon that James had sent along when he met her at the depot proved inadequate for the task of hauling all her baggage, and had to make two trips, heavily loaded each time.

The excitement of getting off the train led the two dogs to raising a real hue and cry. It got so confusing with all the baggage, the yelping dogs, and so forth that James hardly had an opportunity to chat with Anne until they were on their way back to the house in the surry. Following was the gardener driving the spring wagon laden with the luggage, two dogs, and the servant girl.

Annie was quite impressed by the Hulpman house and gave James's arm a little squeeze when it came into view. She knew that she would be staying in that house for several weeks, and was looking forward to it. It was even better than her parents' house back in England. Anne had had no idea that James' house was so nice, and the grounds so neat and spacious.

As everybody was disembarking from the surry and the springwagon, Anne and the servant girl,

Mollie, were trading comments about how strange and wonderful it was that there should be such a place so close to the edge of the wild west.

After the ladies were settled into their quarters, dinner was served. So began a several  week visit in America by the pair from England.

The way in which two people will react to each other is always a question, of course. Sometimes expectations are raised between people who have come to know each other only through correspondence. Oftentimes, those expectations are very unrealistic. We don't know if that was the case with Anne or not, but she apparently was having some difficulty getting used to James. Every day she was around, James grew more and more apprehensive about the whole thing. He just didn't seem to be making the right impression on Anne. And he was right. Anne was deciding that he was a nice young man, but that's as far as it went.

James pulled out all the stops in his campaign to win Anne's heart. He provided fresh flowers for her table each morning catered to every wish that

he guessed she might be having, and was generally doing the best he could. He enlisted the aid of Mollie, the servant, to try to figure out how to make Anne happy. He figured that if Anne was enjoying herself, then she might find herself learning to love him just a tiny part as much as he loved her.

Mollie did what she could to come up with ideas for James. She strongly suggested several times that James take Anne on picnics.

"Oh, Master Hulpman, my Anne dearly loves to go on picnics."

"Picnics, you say?"

"Yes, she loves them. I prepare many such outings for her back in England. She was, in fact, saying on the ship over here that she surely hoped that you would treat her to some nice picnics."

"Well, I shall certainly do that. Thank you, Mollie, for your help."

So James took Anne on one surprise picnic after the other. They went down to the river and out to Blue Grass in James' buggy. Mollie was really very helpful to James in providing him with  information about what kinds of food and drink to take on those picnics. He counted himself lucky that Mollie was able to do that, as well as she knew Anne, and all. He felt a few twinges of guilt, kind of sneaking around Anne that way, but he felt anything was fair in love and war and this was definitely love. Every day Anne was around, James found himself more and more in love.

Unfortunately, though, even the picnics didn't seem to turn the tide in James' favor. Anne grew ever more dissatisfied with life in America and was obviously anxious to go home to England. When James saw that, he grew desperate for an answer to the situation. He appealed once more to Mollie for some advice.

"Master James, I don't know what to tell you. It

is true that my mistress is unhappy here. She knows you are being a most gracious host, but she longs for her home in England. Just last evening she was talking about the need to arrange for passage home."

"But what can I do? I'm afraid that when she leaves here, that shall be the last I shall ever see of her."

"I fear you are right, Master James. I can only suggest you continue showing her a nice time here, and pray that she changes her mind. Perhaps if the weather permits next week, a picnic by the river would be nice."

With that James decided that he would give Anne a picnic that would end them all. He arranged for the finest food available to be taken to the site, along with wine in a large ice-filled bucket. He went so far as to have a fresh bouquet set up there on a snow white table cloth, and sterling silver in its place. He and Mollie labored for several days to be sure that everything was just right. It was, undoubtedly, the finest picnic ever set up in Scott County, either before that day, or since.

As nice as that picnic was, it proved to be of no avail. Anne made her decision. She would return to England the following week. She instructed Mollie to begin preparations for their return.

Anne felt badly about how she had not developed the feelings for James that he obviously had for her.

It was a hard week for James to endure. Only a couple of days after Anne had made that decision James was in the library, trying to divert his mind with some reading.

His eyes followed the words, but his heart wasn't up to the task. In his preoccupation, James didn't hear the door to the library open and close again. He didn't realize, at first, that anyone else was in the room until he felt that small feminine hand on his shoulder. James dared not turn around to look since he was afraid the tears welling up in his eyes would betray the depth of his despair. That hand rested there on his shoulders as if to say "I'm sorry."

Almost as if James's hand had a mind of its own, it raised to touch hers. Perhaps it was the trama of Anne's leaving that caused him to grasp that

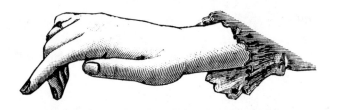

hand with such a special feeling. It seemed that love itself bound those two hands together. James knew his love was incurable. He knew that here was a woman with whom he could gladly spend the last of his days with. Those tears came even closer to the edge of his eyes.

Sadly, James turned to look at Anne.

Sometimes things so dramatic happen to us that we have difficulty believing our own senses. There stood Mollie, the same Mollie that James had spent so much time with lately, conspiring to make Anne happy. There was the Mollie that had worked beside him those long hours arranging activities for he and Anne. James suddenly realized all those hours together had had an effect on him that he was totally unready for. It was so bizarre he could hardly believe it had happened, but it had! James had fallen in love with Mollie! It was Mollie he loved!

Anne felt keenly, the awkward nature of their parting as she prepared to board the train two or three days later. Because of that she tried to confine her conversation with James to safe and routine matters. She even tried to make the moment as light as she could as the conductor was making sure all the baggage had been loaded and getting ready to announce "All-'Board".

"James, there is one thing I should tell you. I probably should have told you this a couple of weeks ago, but I didn't. I should have told you that I have always found eating outside in the woods to be a most distressing thing to do. I simply can't abide picnics. I'm sorry. You prepared some very nice ones for me, and I do appreciate your thoughtfulness. I just don't like picnics at all."

With an audible gasp, James turned to Mollie standing there at his side to bid her mistress good-bye. His unasked question was quickly answered by Mollie's shy smile.

James was probably the happiest Englishman in Iowa as he and Mollie drove back to his home which was soon to be their's together.

VI

THE FLIP OF THE COIN

he whole episode started out in a quite conventional manner. When Loren Welch of Sac City met Patricia Weller from Carroll, he did what any normal red-blooded frontier man would do. He promptly fell in love with her.

The evening when Loren met Patricia there in the Marshall home outside of Sac City was over in what seemed like just a few minutes to Loren. He had never met anyone quite so charming or anywhere near so beautiful or pleasant to be with. It  seemed that Patricia was everything that Loren had ever thought he would want in a woman.

The next couple of weeks involved a flurry of correspondence between the pair. Actually, it was almost all Loren's correspondence with only one short note from Patricia. Loren was so engrossed in his efforts to win the heart of Patricia that it didn't occur to him how one sided that whole relationship was.

Patricia wasn't disinterested, she was simply undecided. She thought Loren was certainly a nice enough fellow, but she certainly wasn't as stricken with him as much as he was with her.

The second of those two weeks following the party at the Marshall house started out pretty much looking up for Loren. Patricia's resistence must have been about broken down from that flurry of letters the first week. She had just almost come to the conclusion that she loved Loren Welch.

This development was greeted warmly by Mr. and Mrs. Weller. The Wellers were of the firm opinion

(82)

that Loren Welch was a prime catch for their daughter, Patricia. Loren was a handsome young

fellow from a good family and had a great future lying in front of him. The issue of getting their three daughters good husbands had been weighing on their minds, so Loren was certainly welcome at their home. They were congratulating themselves over the whole thing and thinking that now all they had to do was to find equally good suitors for Patricia's twin sister Patsy, and the youngest girl, Helen.

But suddenly, and unfortunately, the whole situation blew up in Mr. and Mrs. Weller's faces. Just as quickly as Patricia had decided she would welcome Loren as a suitor, she decided she didn't want to be his girl after all.

Affairs of the heart have always proven to be pretty independent of parental influences and it was no different in this case. Patricia wasn't going to be moved from her position. She simply didn't want Loren Welch as a suitor.

What to do? What to do? Here was a perfectly fine prospect for a son-in-law and the opportunity was about to slip out of sight. It wasn't a prospect that the Wellers relished.

The three Weller girls usually put up a united front in their sometimes stormy relationships with their parents. But this time, both Patsy and Helen joined with their mother and father. They thought that

Loren Weller was simply too good a catch for their sister to let go that easily.

It was Patricia's aunt who first came up with the idea. It seemed so simple and straightforward she could hardly believe her good fortune in having thought of it.

"Philip, I have an idea. Perhaps you could keep Loren Welch in the running even without Patricia."

"What do you mean, sister! If Patricia isn't interested, she isn't interested. That's all there is to it."

"Not really."

"What on Earth do you mean?"

"Well, Philip, you know how Patricia and Patsy are twins. Even if they aren't identical twins, they look so much alike that a lot of your own friends can barely tell them apart."

"Yes, but . . . ."

"It's simple, Philip. Patsy has been green with envy that Patricia could have made such a fine catch. I'm sure she would see that wisdom in kind of changing places with Patricia."

"DO YOU MEAN . . . . ?"

"Now, don't get excited. It makes perfectly good sense.

Even as Philip fussed over "that crazy idea" he recognized that it was just crazy enough that it might work.

"Do you think she would? Where is she? Let's talk to her about it!

So Patsy was summoned, as was her sister, Patricia. The scheme was presented to them to get their opinions. The Wellers and Mr. Weller's sister knew that if even one of the girls objected to the plan, it would fall through.

But they didn't. Patricia thought it would be kind

(86)

of funny and exciting to pull that trick. Besides that, she had taken a sudden interest in the music teacher over at Lake View and was more than willing to help steer Loren's romantic interests away from herself.

Patsy, who was pretty much in awe of that handsome Loren Welch thought it was the greatest idea anyone had ever come up with.

"But wait." Patsy said, "We might be able to convince him that I am the girl he became so infatuated with a couple weeks ago, but it wouldn't do for me to change my name to Patricia. He would eventually figure out we are lying. After all, there can't be two Patricias in the family."

"But, Patsy," Patricia replied. "I told him my name was Pat. I use that name often, as you know. And you could too, if you wanted since it is a nickname for Patsy as well as it is for Patricia. That name would work for you just as well as it does for me."

So the decision was made. Patricia spent the next couple of days recalling every detail of her conversation with Loren a fortnight earlier and coaching Patsy as to exactly what had happened. She described, in detail, the Marshall home where they met; how the rooms were laid out and even the name of Marshall's dog. She told her of the various things they had talked about, and what they had for lunch.

The big night when Loren would be coming to see "Pat" arrived. Patsy wore her own dress, but borrowed Patricia's purse, shoes, and parasol. She even used the same perfume that Patricia did the evening she was up to the Marshall home.

Patricia was going to stay home and allow herself to be seen, but only in a fleeting way. She fixed her hair different so she looked a lot less like "Pat" than Patsy did.

Patsy thought, a couple of times, they maybe it wasn't going to work. She found it necessary in her conversation with Loren to remember something she had no idea of. But she managed. Patsy was even more impressed by Loren than she had been before, and was going to great lengths to successfully step into her sister's shoes.

There were some pretty exciting times that night after Loren left as the two girls talked about Patsy's performance. They went over the events of the evening, and decided that it went rather well and were pretty thrilled over how easy it all was.

Patsy kept up the pretense in the weeks and months that followed. She and Loren hit it off very well. His visits to Carroll became more and more frequent as that romance blossomed and grew.

Then things changed dramatically and suddenly all within the space of a week. Patricia had yet another change of heart. She lost interest in that music teacher over at Lakeview and decided that she could learn to love Loren after all. To complicate matters, it was that same week that Loren proposed to Patsy.

Things got pretty tense as the two girls cried and fussed their way through a twenty-four-hour-a-day argument over the situation. Patricia was of the opinion that they ought to reveal the whole trick to Loren and let him choose. Patsy didn't want to disturb the status quo, of course. Mr. and Mrs. Weller didn't much care which of their girls snagged Loren Welch, just so one of them did.

Patricia tearfully appealed to her parents and finally won out. So it was done.

We can only speculate, of course, at what went through Loren's mind as the story unfolded and he was faced with the need to make a decision. He had really grown to love Pat, but was having difficulty in coming to grips with the issue of who was who and who Pat really was. He was inclined toward Patsy, but at the same time, he felt she had been the one most involved in the trickery.

Actually, Loren soon discovered that he preferred whichever one of the two girls he happened to be with at any given time. Those girls were so much alike, and he was sure he loved somebody, but the poor fellow just couldn't figure out which one it was.

One would think that everybody would have been pretty fed up with the clever ideas of the Wellers, but apparently they weren't, for the next idea they came up with was acceptable to everybody.

They would flip a coin. Or rather, they would all get together while a lawyer friend of the family would officiate, doing the actual flipping. So it was arranged.

The whole operation was to take place at the girls'
home in Carroll. Loren was there, two friends of
his, the girls, their sister, their parents, and the
lawyer. The Wellers even furnished a bottle of vin-
tage wine to mark the occassion.

Apparently the whole thing was done in a festive
mood. The girls had resigned their contentious
positions and had agreed to live gracefully with
the results of the flip. And surprisingly Loren was
glad to have an easy way out of having to make
a decision.

The lawyer played his role to the hilt, with great fanfare defining the ground rules and getting all the principals to agree.

The lawyer even used some of the words and phrases from the gentlemanly art of dueling in order to borrow some of the romance of an earlier time.

After the due amount of pomp and ceremony the fellow spun that coin up into the air and slapped his hand over it as it hit the table, covering it from everybody's sight. All that, of course, served to impact to the procedure the appropriate amount of drama and excitement.

"What is it?" little Helen said almost under breath.

All the people around the table quietly looked at that hand as the lawyer lifted it up away from the coin. The lives of several of the onlookers would be profoundly affected by the position of that coin under that hand.

It had already been agreed that if it was "heads", the prize would go to Patricia. If it was "tails", Patsy would wed Loren.

The following month, Mr. and Mrs. Weller were the proud parents-in-law of Loren Welch, little Helen was the ring bearer, Patricia the maid of honor and Patsy the blushing bride.

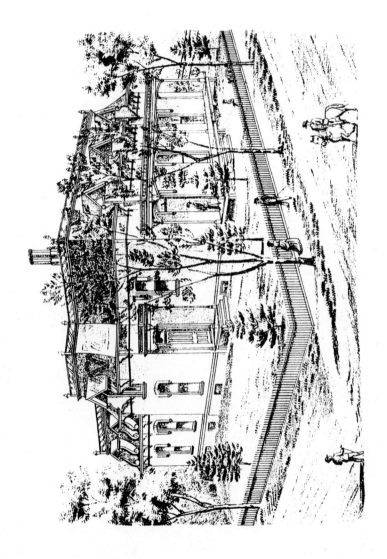

VII

WHAT COULD HAVE BEEN

ll of us know that romance often travels a rocky road. This has been true in the past as much as it is now. This fact is more than amply demonstrated by the history of this old house here in Iowa just one block off the main street in Sigourney. It is one of the most embellished buildings in the state.

The house is what is known as the Woodin House in Sigourney, and is shown on page 94.

As ornate as the Woodin House is, as well shown in the illustration, it seems even much more so in real life. One of my first thoughts when I saw it was that the interior must be really unbelievable if the builder went to so much bother to gussy up the outside.

Strangely enough, though, the inside is not only plain, but remarkably so. The inside of that house is much plainer that many houses less pretentious on the outside. Why is that?

The answer lies in the old love story that goes back a hundred and twenty years, now.

There are a number of versions of the love story associated with the Woodin House. They pretty much agree in the basics, but differ in terms of many of the details. The story that follows seems to be the one that the greatest number of people I talked to agree upon.

It all started in 1870 when Mr. Woodin met and

fell in love with a young lady whose name the records don't reveal. In the interest of readability, I am going to take the liberty of giving this young lady a name. We'll call her Barbara.

Mr. Woodin was a man of some resources and influence in the community since he was a respected business man in Sigourney. While he did not run it himself, he had majority interest in a lumber yard that supplied the needs of the townspeople and those on the surrounding farms for many miles around.

The story goes that Mr. Woodin had a beautiful two passenger surrey that he and Barbara would drive down to the North Skunk River where they would have delightful picnics. The surrey was Mr. Woodin's hobby for which he spared no expense. The harness was reported to be generously decorated with bright hardware, but of sterling silver rather than the more common nickel plated brass. The harness graced the backs of two jet black and perfectly matched Morgan horses. One

can only imagine how proud he must have been, driving that magnificent team in his luxurious surrey while taking a beautiful young lady to a picnic on a summer afternoon.

Mr. Woodin was apparently stricken so severely by cupid's arrows that he wrote poems to his Barbara telling of his love.

It seems that this romantic relationship between these two went rather well for several months, until 1871 when the pair had a falling out.

Whatever the difficulty was, it proved to be permanent, with Barbara stalking off and going her own way.

Aside from these folks going on a lot of picnics before their breakup, we know little of their relationship. One thing we do know, however, is that they had some rather detailed discussions about the kind of house they would be building as soon as they got married. It seems that Barbara had had some rather definite ideas of what she wanted in a house and one of them was lots and lots of ornamentation, both inside and out.

The story goes that the pair had spent quite a lot of time and effort in planning their new home, even including such things as the kind of grass seed to use on the lawn and the exact colors of the  home, even down to the colors of the little nooks and crannies of the ornamentation she had her heart so set on.

When the romance broke up, that put an end to

all sorts of plans, including those involved in building that dream house. Usually, of course, all those drawings and sketches lovingly made while

the couple had lounged in that surrey would have been pitched without any hesitation. They would have been too much a reminder of a romance gone sour. For some reason, however, Mr. Woodin kept those. Maybe his instincts as a lumber yard owner prevented him from tossing them. But, then again, maybe he had in mind to employ those plans for the use they were ultimately put. We don't know.

In any event, Barbara soon met a new suitor and left a very disappointed Mr. Woodin to running his businesses and tending to his fancy driving rig.

This new suitor eventually won Barbara's hand in marriage. There was a grand wedding held there in Sigourney, the likes of which hadn't been seen around those parts for quite a while.

After Barbara's big wedding, she and her new husband settled down right there in Sigourney.

This couple built their own new home on the south side of town. It would be interesting to know if they purchased their building materials from the lumber yard in which Mr. Woodin had an interest. While we don't know that, we do know that the house this couple built was a particularly nice one. Perhaps Mr. Woodin saw some familiar features in it since Barbara undoubtedly had a hand in its planning also.

Meanwhile, Mr. Woodin, being a man of substance, was fair game for the eligible and unmarried ladies in Sigourney. Apparently he was able to overcome his grief over losing Barbara enough to pay attention to some of them, for shortly he found another one and married her.

Shortly after Barbara and her husband's house was built in 1872, another new home went up in Sigourney. Mr. Wooden was building it and it appeared to be the exact house that he and Barbara had worked so long in planning.

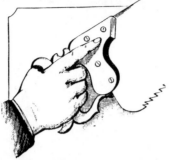

While Mr. Woodin might well have had no such idea in mind, the story circulating around Sigourney in 1872 was that he had built the house exactly as he and Barbara had planned it just for the purpose of saying "See what you could have had." Apparently Woodin's house outshone even the very nice one that Barbara and her husband had built. The ornamentation in the Woodin house that Barbara had had her heart set on was so extreme that it was considered, at that time, to be the last word in good taste.

That extreme ornamentation did not carry through to the inside of the house, however. It was very plain inside. The woodwork was of a soft wood rather than the oak or walnut usually used for houses as expensive as Mr. Woodlin had put up. That woodwork was inferior to that used in many much more common houses that

(102)

were built at the time.

The installation of that common wood work seemed to confirm, in the minds of many, that it was a house built simply for Barbara to see. People knew that she would probably never be in the interior of the house. So, they reasoned, Mr. Woodin had spent his money only on the outside of the house, the only part that Barbara would see.

There was supposed to have been a lot of tongue wagging over the whole issue.

The available records about the house and the family don't address the issue of what Mrs. Woodin thought of her husband building a house in such a strange manner, with an excess amount of ornamentation on the exterior and virtually none on the inside. If the home was built for the alleged reason of simply showing Barbara what could have been, did Mrs. Woodin know it? Didn't she have anything to say about how it was built?

It would be fun to know the answers to those questions. If Mrs. Woodin ever got wind of those rumers, I'll bet her husband got his ear bent over the whole thing.

The years haven't been real kind to the Woodin

house. It kind of hangs and sags where it shouldn't. The house isn't in a shape to impress Barbara or any other girl with "what could have been." But, even at that, it is the only remaining one of the players of that drama in Sigourney of a hundred and twenty years ago.

VIII

WIDOW CUMMINS

hen Alyce Cummins of near Reading, Pennsylvania lost her husband to smallpox while she was but twenty-five years old back in 1884, she was devasted almost beyond her ability to cope with the situation.

She and Wayne had been married only a few
weeks when that tragedy visited them, leaving
Alyce alone and expecting a baby when she was
still a very young woman.

Her marriage with Wayne had been so brief that
she had hardly gotten to meet any of his people.
She had met his mother, but not yet his father or
brother.

That marriage that had been entered into with
such love and bright promises was gone. Gone too,
was Alyce's desire to ever be married again. The
hurt was more than she was willing to risk having
to bear a second time.

The tidy sum of money that Wayne had inherited
from a grandparent became Alyce's. But that was
small compensation for the loss she had suffered.

She would have gladly have given that money up a million times for the opportunity to have her husband back, if only for a day. She had, in fact, dreamt just that on several occassions after Wayne's death.

Such dreams, however, cannot be, and Alyce had to put her life back together and keep going. She had to do that for their yet unborn child, if nothing else.

It was common in Pennsylvania, as well as other parts of the country in those days following the Civil War for folks to "pick up" and "go west" to that huge land beyond the frontier. It was a promise of a new life for individuals as

well as for entire families.

Alyce Cummins had no interest in seeking her fortune in the West, but that seemed like an opportunity for her to get away from the painful memories of Reading where everybody and everything would remind her of her husband, Wayne. So, without a lot of hesitation, Alyce headed west.

She looked forward to the trip down the Ohio River and then over land from the Mississippi River. She also looked forward to the excitement of a new

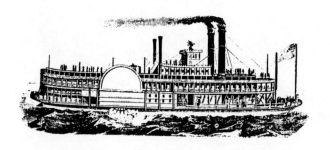

country and new ways of helping her forget. She decided to go as far as necessary to find some nice moutains. She had never known mountains before and thought that would be something kind of special.

Alyce Cummins never got to the mountains of the west. In fact, she never got beyond Woodbury County, Iowa. Why she choose to settle here in Iowa is a mystery. While a journal she kept reveals to us many of the details of her trip and even her day-to-day thoughts, it doesn't tell us why she chose to stay here in Iowa rather than continuing on out west where she could live near the mountains as she had looked forward to doing.

The home shown on Page 106 was built according to Alyce's specifications. Her jounal hints as to why she decided to build a house considerably larger than she and her baby would need. Apparently the house was very much like the one she had grown up in back in Pennsylvania.

Alyce settled in quite quickly in her new house and busied herself in the countless tasks of picking out rugs, the curtains, paint for the walls, and what to put in the garden.

(111)

All that was faithfully entered into her journal. Those yellowed pages are over a hundred years old now, of course.

Anyone who has ever completed the task of finishing off a house and furnishing it knows that it can be a big job, and Alyce threw herself into it, perhaps to help forget. She needed to forget that lonely grave back in Pennsylvania.

By this time little Jacob was born, so it took a lot of Alyce's time to take care of the baby while she was working on the house.

The three years that followed were busy ones for the young widow. Being a strikingly beautiful lady, Alyce had many opportunities for romantic relationships with fellows there in Sioux City. She was quite impartial in her response to that. She treated them all with equal coolness, having no interest in ever considering marriage again. The word soon got around the community that, while Alyce Cummins was a beautiful young lady, the fellows might as well save their efforts. She simply wasn't interested.

When Abe Collins came to Sioux City he was really impressed with Alyce and didn't feel inclined to believe the other fellows who insisted that he might as well forget Alyce Cummins. With a confidence born of youth, Abe proceeded to "court" the young

widow. The fact that Alyce wasn't interested didn't sway him one bit. He thought Alyce was about the nicest thing he had ever seen and he wasn't about to give up without giving a good go at it.

Abe wrangled a few opportunities to chat briefly with Alyce on the street, at the General store, or wherever else he could engineer a "chance" meeting. It didn't take long, in those conversations, for Abe to develop a real admiration for Alyce.

Early in this situation, Alyce did nothing to encourage Abe. She, in fact, did what she could to discourage him, just like she had all the others.

Meanwhile, Abes admiration grew quickly to fondness, then to love.

Abe's quick smile and winning ways eventually proved too much for her. She liked that young fellow and enjoyed their visits, even as she pretended impatience with him. Those "chance" visits on the street and at the General Store became summer evenings spent on Alyce's front porch where the pair would sit and keep an eye on Jacob. Those were soon changed to "just friends" outings to play tennis, go horseback riding, and so forth.

Abe was good for Alyce. Those eyes that hadn't sparkled for many months except with tears, soon grew lighter and laughter came quickly to her again.

Alyce was surprised, by fall, to find that she not only looked forward to Abe coming to visit, but that she was also very fond of him. That fondness survived even Abe's reluctance to talk about his life before coming west to Iowa. Repeated questions by Alyce were to no avail. He always gave her evasive answers and little of any substance. Alyce thought less of that odd situation than one would today since many of the men who had "come west" had done so in order to get a new start in life, and to leave an old one behind. Many men were awfully close-lipped about their pasts.

It would be weeks yet before Alyce was to find out that Abe had fled his hometown back east and had changed his name to avoid a confrontation with a murderous bully back there. That man had already murdered one man and had threatened to kill Abe.

Abe had decided that the best way to keep his identity secret was to reveal it to absolutely no one. That way it would not be necessary to make decisions as to who should know who he was and who shouldn't. That policy extended even to the lovely young widow with whom he had, by now, fallen hopelessly in love.

Abe and Alyce got along just fine and found themselves spending more and more time together. Alyce's fondness soon grew to love. This surprised her since she had been so sure that there could never be anyone who could take Wayne's place.

It surprised the other fellows in town too, who had watched that stranger, Abe, come to town and sweep Widow Cummins right into a romance.

Folks in their twenties don't find themselves in love very long without something happening. And the something that happened was that the pair set a date for their marriage the following May.

Keeping a secret from a girlfriend or a boyfriend is a whole lot different than keeping one from a husband or wife. So, prior to the wedding, Abe Collins told Alyce about the incident with the bully back east and how he had changed his name from Walter Cummins to Abe Collins. He told her about his family which consisted of his parents and a brother, Wayne, who had died not much earlier of smallpox.

(116)

He had just gotten started telling about how Wayne had gotten married, then immediately contacted the dreaded smallpox and died.

Abe's story came to an abrupt halt, however, when he realized that Alyce was distraught almost to the point of fainting.

Abe's anxious questions asking Alyce what the problem was went unanswered for several minutes until Alyce could compose herself between sobs to tell Abe that she had been that widowed bride of Wayne Cummins'. She had been his brother's wife!

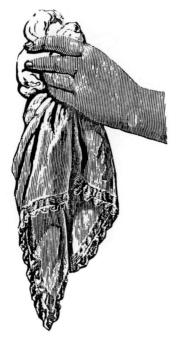

That evening was an exciting one in which Abe and Alyce shared information about their lives that they hadn't before.

It took the couple a little time to get accustomed to the fact that Alyce and Abe's brother had been married, but their own marriage took place as scheduled in May anyway. It was a marriage that united two families that had been so united before.

The three Collins boys that came along over the next few years were all spittin' images of the Cummins family and they fit right in with their older half-brother Jacob.

IX

BERNICE'S CHANGE

 drian Hotler, who built the Hotler home just outside of Des Moines started that home in 1894 and finished it in 1897. He built it in anticipation of marrying Bernice Swayton from over in Iowa City.

Adrian didn't let the fact that his bride-to-be was a totally spoiled brat slow down his marriage plans. While love might not be blind, it sure has a bad

case of poor eyesight. Adrian was able to overlook that one single fault of her's. In fact, he wouldn't even admit to his friends that she was a thoughtless and inconsiderate person.

"After all, none of us are perfect." he would be apt to say.

Adrian was so much in love with Bernice that he would have forgiven her being spoiled or anything else. He just plain had a bad case of it.

Bernice, on the other hand, was the type of person who was willing to remember every slight, real or imagined. She made note of every error and fault that Adrian or anyone else ever made. She was the kind of person who would keep accurate count of every favor given and every one owed.

There were lots of things Adrian had done in this world to earn him a fine girl who would bring him happiness. But nothing he had ever done was bad enough for fate to saddle him with a spoiled brat like Bernice.

Adrian charged forth with his plans to marry. Fate, however, wasn't going to let it be so simple. It had a couple of bad cards to deal first.

The house that Adrian was having built in readiness for the marriage was an ambitious one for a man of modest resources, but it was what Bernice wanted, so it was what Bernice was going to get. Not once did Adrian think of anything other than  what his beautiful Bernice wanted. In his blindness of love for her, he thought of nothing but her.

In an effort to keep the costs of that house down as much as possible, Adrian was doing a lot of the work himself.

It was a rather large house and the work had drug on for months and months. Adrian was more than willing, however, to use every spare minute he had to work on a home for him and his Bernice. It was truly a labor of love.

On ocassion, Bernice would stop by the house and find enough things wrong with it that it would require Adrian having to undo some of his work and do it all over again. He would do that without complaint. Love is not only blind, it's deaf as well.

It was on a Sunday afternoon and Adrian was working on the house. He was sprawled out on the floor of what was going to be the parlor, taking some measurements up inside the fireplace, preparatory to installing an iron damper plate.

In his efforts to get that job done, Adrian had forgotten that the heavy marble mantel over the fireplace entrance was not securely affixed to the wall. It was simply sitting up there, little more than balanced on the supports. That thick stone slab, well over ten feet long and a foot and a half wide, had taken six strong men to lift it up over the fireplace, for it was a heavy thing.

Maybe it was Adrian's working there in the fireplace, or perhaps it was simply time for fate to dictate that that piece of marble should fall.

Whatever the reason, it came crashing down with a thud that the neighbors on both sides of Adrian's house heard.

In fact, it was one of those neighbors who came over to Adrian's to investigate and found the poor fellow pinned to the floor, securely held in place by that several hundred pound piece of marble. It laid across both legs. Even then, it was obvious to the neighbor that Adrian was severely injured. He was unconscious and the blood from his crushed legs was already staining the oak floor he had so lovingly laid down himself.

The neighbor summoned help immediately, so it was just a few minutes until men were there to lift the mantel off so the doctor could examine and help poor Adrian.

Adrian Hotler survived that terrible accident but not without paying an awful price. He lost both legs. They were amputated that day just above the knees. That, of course, sentenced him to a life in a wheelchair.

Such a thing is always a tragedy, but seems particulairly cruel when it happens to a young person with his life still ahead of him.

Society, as a whole, took less responsibility for the care of the disabled back then then it does now. It was assumed by everyone that Adrian would be faced with the need to depend on the generosity of his friends and relatives for his very livelihood from then on. There was apparently very little thought given to any role that Bernice would play in Adrian's life. Folks knew she would be leaving as soon as it was possible to do so. Girls like Bernice were takers. Givers, like Adrian were obviously no longer a candidate for marriage when he would no longer be able to give. Folks figured that with the likes of Bernice, he probably wasn't even a candidate for friendship with her.

Adrian had time to think a lot about his future as he lie there in his bed recovering from the accident and the amputations. He had decided that what he should do is to leave the house in its semi-finished state, move into it and go from there. He figured that he would be able to stave off going to the poorhouse for a while. The owner of a local general store had offered him the opportunity to clerk part time. Adrian figured that he could do that, some hand woodworking, and tutoring.

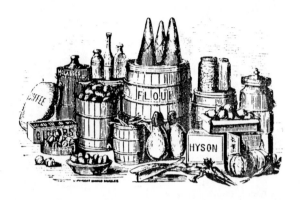

These weren't the sort of plans that are pleasant to make, but fate had dealt its hand, and Adrian had to live with it. With a thin and mirthless laugh, Adrian contrasted those plans with the ones he had been making so shortly before that had included marriage to Bernice and finishing the house to a nice home for the two of them.

Bernice had been to see Adrian several times as he lie in his bed recovering. He had been warned, however, by several of his friends that she would undoubtedly soon stop those visits. Adrian was convinced that he would soon see the last of her. His friends were glad that he was realistic enough that he could see that. They gently pointed out that love is sometimes foolish, but the real world now had to be faced.

So one afternoon found Adrian in a real state of agitation when Bernice came to visit. For she had the air about her of one who was about ready to say something important. Adrian knew full well what it was. He knew she would be telling him that day that it was all over with.

"Adrian, there's something we need to talk about . . . . . . talk . . . . we need to talk about."

"Yes, Bernice."

"Well, I don't know how to say . . . . I don't know how to say this, but we . . . . . . "

Adrian suddenly felt especially saddened. Here he was about to be told it was all over, and Bernice just couldn't bring herself to say the words. It spite of what he was going through, he did love her and felt sorry for her difficulty in  telling him those terrible words. He felt like blurting out something about how it was simply a matter of telling him that she wouldn't be seeing him anymore. A thousand thoughts rushed through his head, but his tongue gave voice to none of them.

"What is it, Bernice?"

Somehow, Bernice found her voice and continued.

"Well, Adrian, I hate to be difficult about this, but I'm convinced that the wheelchair that you are

(127)

thinking about ordering from the catalog isn't going to work. I . . ."

Adrian's look of shock temporarily stopped Bernice's words. He thought it odd that she would concern herself with such things as the kind of wheelchair that he would have.

But she continued.

"I know that wheelchair is too wide to fit up there on the sanctuary of the church. I've been studying the catalog and I've run across one that is just a little bit narrower. It also seems to be a little nicer wheelchair and will cost no more than the one you planned on. We are going to have to watch our money, now, you know."

 Adrian looked at Bernice, completely perplexed.

"What are you talking about, Bernice?"

"What I'm saying, Dear, is that I think we need to look at a different wheelchair and get it ordered in time for the wedding."

"Wedding?"

"Yes." she teased. "You haven't forgotten that we are getting married, have you?"

"But Bernice. We can't . . . . You would not want . . . . . . what I mean is . . . . . "

(128)

It was then that Bernice realized what Adrian had been thinking.

"Adrian."

"Yes?"

Adrian felt a firmness and resolve in Bernice's hand as she took his in her's and told him of her full intention to stay with him as they had agreed.

That conversation in Adrian's room was interrupted by the doctor coming in to visit him.

Adrian's mind was in a whirl as he tried to answer the doctor's questions, but his mind was struggling to comprehend what he had just heard.

Bernice proved all those people wrong. She pitched in and finished the house with the help of lots of friends and neighbors. This time, though, the plans were made for a different kind of house. No longer was it to be the plaything of a spoiled and self-indulgent young lady. Some modifications were made to convert the house to a boarding house with the extra space going for income-producing bedrooms. The kitchen was enlarged to make room for the extra large tables and iceboxes necessary for a boarding house.

Bernice had it in her head that he could run a boarding house as well as anyone else. Time proved her to be right. Within a year the house was completely filled with boarders, and stayed that way for many years.

Adrian did do the clerking at the general store part time and he did run a successful and profitable tutoring business there at the boarding house. Those plus the income from those rooms provided the Hotlers with a quite adequate income for their entire lives.

The Hotler children, all seven of them, grew up in a home with love and respect. Never once did they ever consider their father to be disabled. They saw him run his life successfully with the help of his wife, Bernice.

Perhaps there is as much wisdom in love as there is foolishness. Perhaps love can see things that a blindfold can't hide.

X

MISS HELEN PETERSON

 liff and Brad Harner were brothers only a year apart in age, so it comes as no surprise that the pair were highly competitive. They grew up having to work out who got what and usually scrapping over the decision. Things got a bit tight on occassion when Mr. Harner had spells of going without work. When that would happen, the boys would have to fight over the sizes of their respective piles of potatoes or number of spoons of gravey.

But it wasn't only food that offered opportunities for the boys to argue and scrap. Their clothes, who got to sleep where, and the dividing up of the household chores were all fertile grounds for the boys to argue.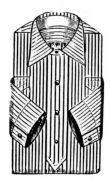

Cliff and Brad about outgrew all that fussing and arguing by the time they got to be in their early twenties. That is, they pretty well got over it until Helen Peterson came into their lives in 1904. Helen was the daughter of a couple that came to the large Harner home as boarders.

Now, those two boys had always viewed the whole boarder thing as a pain in the neck. The need for them to accomodate an endless number of boarders had always been a bit of a bother, and they resented the economic need to take all these people into their home.

But with the arrival of Helen Peterson, all that changed. They decided that taking in boarders wasn't such a bad idea at all. Helen Peterson was just about the nicest looking girl that either one of the boys had ever seen.

Suddenly the logistics at the dinner table became a big issue. Central to the whole thing, of course, was who got to sit by Helen. That particular question was finally put to rest with a compromise. Each of the boys got to sit on one side of the object of their affection.

The pair, of course, kept up a running battle over who would have the priviledge of accompanying Miss Peterson from the dining room table to the parlor at the end of the dinner meal. And who would get to serve that beautiful young lady desert was always a bone of contention.

That bickering for the attentions of Helen soon got more serious as the boys grew from infatuation to love. Both of those brothers fell in love with Helen hard enough to jar what little good sense they had right out of them. Things got pretty tense around the Harner boarding house on several occasions as those boys vied for the attention of Helen, almost coming to blows more than once.

Both Cliff and Brad sensed that this was a whole lot bigger than the things they had been accustomed to fighting about, and it was starting to drive a wedge between the two of them.

It would be a mistake to call this situation a love triangle. It wasn't a three way thing at all. There were only two people in love, Cliff and Brad. Both these boys were hopelessly in love with Helen. She, however, cared not a bit about either one of them. All they were doing was making complete fools out of themselves over her.

While Helen didn't have any special feelings for either one of the boys, she did enjoy the novelty of being fought over. She would work one of the fellows against the other in an effort to keep the whole thing going. If it appeared that things might calm down, Helen would figure out some way to pour fuel on the fire. She managed to keep everything in a general uproar as only a woman can do.

(136)

As is common to affairs of the heart, the whole thing didn't run on an even keel. The boys became increasingly enamored with Helen and even more out of sorts with each other. Pretty soon it got to the point that even Helen knew the issue had to be resolved. She decided that she had better figure out which one she liked the most and would reward him with the opportunity to be her boyfriend.

Since Helen could take or leave either of them, she made her decision almost as if it were based on the roll of the dice. Without any more thought than that she decided she would prefer that Cliff be her boyfriend.

Not being content to make a choice and then letting it go at that, Helen couldn't pass up the opportunity to do a little power romancing and plotted that Brad should have to hurt as much as possible. So she proceeded to initiate a whispering campaign to discredit and embarrass brother Brad.

Cliff pressed his advantage as soon as it became obvious that he was about to win the heart of the beautiful Helen Peterson. He was thrilled to know that he had prevailed and let his brother know that Helen was not only beautiful, but was an excellent judge of character. Flush with success, it didn't occur to Cliff that not only was Helen no judge of character, but didn't have any herself.

Cliff's secret rendevous with Helen under the grape arbor that first afternoon of his victory should have

been an idyllic and romantic sort of thing. It was there, however, that Cliff learned that Helen was not only stabbing Brad in the back, but was twisting the knife on him. The heated argument that ensued between Cliff and Helen left but one person in love that day, Cliff's brother Brad.

When Cliff got to Brad and told him what had been going on, that left nobody in love that day at all.

Both fellows ignored Helen Peterson thereafter until the day she and her parents left the Harner Boarding House a few weeks later.

I'm sure this old mansion shown on page 132 has had other romances associated with it. I'll also bet that almost any of them would prove to have been more satisfactory than the one involving Cliff, Brad, and Helen.

XI

GOLDEN HAIR

 n 1889, a farmer who lived outside of Buffalo fell in love. That fact, in itself, was not particularly remarkable. After all, men fall in love somewhere just about every day. What was remarkable was how hard he fell. Jesse Hinton loved the object of his affections more than any other man had ever loved before. At least he was convinced that he did. It sure seemed that way to him.

Unfortunately, the situation was a bit more complicated than Jesse and Laura would have preferred. The fact is, they were both married; but not to each other.

Jesse's love for beautiful, beautiful Laura was one that knew no bounds. In those

(141)

stolen moments when they would meet in secret, Jesse would hold her and feel that he was at least twelve feet tall. His head would be aswirl with conflicting emotions. He felt his entire world was so complete, yet he knew he was holding the wife of another man in his arms. Jesse would bury his face in her golden hair and dream of what might have been, and what might yet be. He would half

close his eyes and the sun would make tiny sparkles in her hair; sparkles that seemed to mock him, even as they so captivated his heart. Jesse Hinton had a pretty bad case of it alright.

Jesse's love was returned by Laura. He was fortunate in that since he loved her so much he would not have been able to face each day had she spurned his total adoration of her.

(142)

Poor Jesse was so much in love that he dared not face the many problems that would have to be solved in order to make Laura his wife. He dared not, perhaps for fear that those problems might prove to be insoluable.

The weeks and months passed by. By some miracle, Jesse found that his love for Laura grew with each day. Every day he loved her more than he did the one before. Yet each day was one more that he had to live without her at his side at his wife.

The lovers would meet in secret places. They would often spend a stolen hour in the woods, away from the prying eyes of others. Jesse long-ed, however, to escape the need for secrecy. He heard of the writings of a young radical in Concord, Massachusetts, by the name of Henry David Thoreau. Thoreau had written, a few years earlier:

> *"The mass of men*
> *lead lives of*
> *quiet desperation."*

Jesse took that to heart, burdened by the need to keep his agony to himself. He felt like he was nothing but a caged animal with no way to turn. On occasion he would even dream that his terrible

secret formed bars around him and he was reduced to hours of ceaseless pacing. Then he would
wake up and find himself doing just that.

Jesse wanted Laura so much, yet he was afraid he
would never have her. Even she would speak of
the difficulties of their marrying. Perhaps, he
thought, she considered the obstacles too great to
overcome.

Jesse's desperation grew with the passage of time.
He schemed and thought; he planned and figured.
Whenever Laura would speak of the problems and
urge him to find happiness without her, it was as
if the corner he was backed into crowded him even
closer.

This obsession with his new-found love was

apparently Jesse's eventual undoing. He knew his way around horses, and should have known better than to walk too close behind that mean bay gelding he had. Jesse was probably lost in thought about Laura that day, as he was on all days. That gelding saw his opportunity and took it.

That kick was fatal, and Jesse probably never knew what hit him. The gelding finally got his licks in and Jesse was finally relieved of his agony of not having his beautiful Laura as his own.

Laura had to pretend to feel only the loss of a neighbor. She claimed an illness the day of the funeral so she didn't have to go through that. Jesse was appropriately buried in the local cemetery, and life promised to continue much the same as it had in the humdrum days before Jesse and Laura loved each other.

The story of this couple wasn't over yet, however.

There was a couple of chapters not yet written. One of these was in regard to an incident that happened late one night after Laura had drifted off to sleep. She awoke with the distinct impression of having heard a familiar sound. It was the snip-snip-snip-snip of a pair of scissors. She was, in fact, half awakened twice that night, hearing those scissors snipping close by. In her drowsy state, she thought little of it until the next morning. Shortly after she got up, she was washing her face. As Laura looked in the mirror, she was shocked to see that a large portion of her hair was gone. It was as if it had been cut with scissors.

It was then she recalled distinctly what she had heard that night.

Laura knew it couldn't be, yet it wasn't her imagination. There was no mistaking the fact that some of her hair had been cut off in the night. There was the evidence right there in the mirror.

 Try as she could to understand just what had happened, it was to no avail. It had happened, and that was all there was to it.

Laura repaired her tresses by cutting some off of the other side, and smoothing the whole thing out. She decided just to accept the whole thing as one of those things that simply couldn't be explained.

A few weeks went by before the final episode of this tale was revealed.

A heavy and sudden spring rain caused the creek bank at the cemetery to drop into the swollen waters. The damage at the edge of the cemetery was so extensive that three of the coffins were partly exposed. One of these was the relatively new one containing the earthly remains of Jessie Hinton. New as that coffin was, it had already started to disintegrate. The decision was therefore made to place Jesse's remains in a new coffin and to put it in a portion of the cemetery less vulnerable to flood damage.

Some of the local men proceeded to make the transfer. Since Buffalo was but a small town, most everyone knew everybody else. In fact, two of the workmen on the cemetery crew had been to Jesse's funeral. They both recalled that Jesse had been laid out in the traditional and formal manner practiced back in those days. His arms had been placed straight down along his sides.

These men were shocked to see that Jesse's arms weren't like they had been when he had been buried. Rather than lying there along his sides,

proper like, they were bent and his hands were up to his face. In those hands were grasped several locks of golden hair.

As the men stood there and silently studied the situation, a cloud passed from over the sun and the bright spring light shone into the interior of the coffin. The sunlight illuminated those tresses, making tiny sparkles of light in that golden hair. The sparkles danced quickly back and forth as a gentle April breeze moved those locks. The dancing sparkles seemed to mock their captor just as they had captivated him in those stolen moments of months earlier.

XII

LUCINDA

t comes as no surprise that there should be a love story in Stoney Hollow.

Stoney Hollow is a truly beautiful series of ravines and high bluffs a few miles north of Burlington. The creek wanders through there, making lots of twists and turns. It's as if the creek were reluctant to leave the hollow. Those cool and deep ravines offer a welcome respite on a hot August day.

The love story of Stoney Hollow, however, ended in tragedy on a hot August day many years ago. The best estimate seems to be that it was in the late 1870s or early 1880s.

The daughter of a local farmer was courted by many of the boys in the neighborhood. The more daring of them asked to be allowed to visit Lucinda. The rest simply suffered through the pangs of love unspoken and unreturned.

Beautiful young Lucinda had skin the hue of an acorn and hair the color of a jet black raven. It was so black that it almost appeared to be a metallic blue.

Lucinda's father knew that his fine farm, along with his daughter's beauty would enable him to arrange a very advantageous marriage for her. He had visions of a very generous dowry or even the opportunity to combine, through marriage, his farm with that of another of equal or better quality.

(152)

Lucinda's father looked forward with some real anticipation to how he was going to turn her beauty into a real advantage for the family.

His dreams, however, ran headlong into trouble. Trouble came in the form of a local suitor whose family enjoyed neither prestige or property. This ambitious father could almost ignore that annoyance until he learned that the lad and Lucindia were having rendezvous there in Stoney Hollow. In those days it was known as Sherfey's Glen.

Lucinda's father learned that his daughter and the ne'er-do-well would walk along the hilltops to meet in a secret place in the glen.

Lucinda was, of course, ordered to stop seeing the young man. That accomplished nothing more than to move the date of the planned elopement of the young couple up a few weeks. The couple conspired to meet at their secret place a couple of days later, then leave together.

He was to bring a horse and buggy and she was to bring whatever she could carry of her things that she would need on their trip.

Their plan was that they would travel all night so as to be as far away from Stoney Hollow as they could get by daybreak.

The plan was well thought out. The ne'er-do-well was to wrap the horses hooves and the buggy wheels in grain sacks so as to obscure their tracks they would make in the moist dirt road. The couple had hidden some food and other provisions in an iron box down by the creek there in the hollow.

They knew that if they traveled by night and hid during the days, they could be a hundred miles away in a short time.

Lucinda could hardly get through that last day. Her need to pretend that it was just another day was almost more than she could handle. That night she left her home and family for what she thought would be forever. Taking that now-familiar path over the hills to their rendezvous, she arrived and waited for her lover to appear. She waited, in fact,  most of the night for the muffled sound of that horse and buggy. It was in vain. He never arrived.

Sick with worry and fear, Lucinda returned home and crept back into her room, and then to bed.

It was the following day that the community was alive with the news that the ne'er-do-well had run off with a yellow-haired girl from over by the river.

Lucinda's feet carried her rapidly to that secret spot. Her tired and tear-swollen eyes closed forever as she plunged off the edge of one of those high limestone bluffs

For years after that terrible day, the ghost of a beautiful young girl could be seen running along the hilltops in Stoney Hollow on hot summer nights.

(155)

Through the years, passers-by would often see small lights moving about in the area of that fatal limestone bluff. Many scoffed at this and said they were just fireflies. Unlike fireflies, however, these lights were blue and would not go off and on such as will the lights from those strange little insects.

On each anniversary of that fateful night someone would be able to hear the sounds of a girl running along the hilltops. It was almost as if the ghost of little Lucinda had never quite accepted that fact that her lover would fail to come for her that night.

Today there is no one left alive who remembers

the site of that home that Lucinda left and returned to on that night so many years ago. The passions of those young lovers of over a hundred years
ago are long since cooled, and only the hills
remain.

EPILOGUE

So hot August nights in Stoney Hollow hear yet,
the sounds of a lover of over a century ago.

And those sad words "....... it might have been."
echo through an old house in Sigourney and a
coffin in Buffalo.

But other Iowa loves have yielded more mortal
results as grandchildren and great-grandchildren
of the players leaf through old family albums yet
today.

If you have enjoyed this book, perhaps you would enjoy others from Quixote Press.

GHOSTS OF THE MISSISSIPPI RIVER
Mpls. to Dubuque by Bruce Carlson . . . . paperback $9.95

GHOSTS OF THE MISSISSIPPI RIVER
Dubuque to Keokuk by Bruce Carlson . . . . . paperback $9.95

GHOSTS OF THE MISSISSIPPI RIVER
Keokuk to St. Louis by Bruce Carlson . . . . . paperback $9.95

RIVER SHARKS & SHENAGANS
by Netha Bell . . . . paperback $9.95

HOW TO TALK MIDWESTERN
by Robert Thomas . . . . paperback $7.95

GHOSTS OF DES MOINES COUNTY, IOWA
by Bruce Carlson . . . . hardback $12.00

JACK KING VS. DETECTIVE MC KENZIE
by Netha Bell . . . . paperback $9.95

GHOSTS OF ROCK ISLAND COUNTY, ILLINOIS
by Bruce Carlson . . . . hardback $12.95

GHOSTS OF THE AMANA COLONIES
by Lori Erickson . . . . paperback $9.95

GHOSTS OF NORTHEAST IOWA
by Ruth Hein and Vicky Hinsenbrock . . . . . paperback $9.95

GHOSTS OF POLK COUNTY, IOWA
by Tom Welch . . . . paperback $9.95

GHOSTS OF THE IOWA GREAT LAKES
by Bruce Carlson . . . . paperback $9.95

MEMOIRS OF A DAKOTA HUNTER
by Gary Scholl . . . . paperback $9.95

LOST AND BURIED TREASURE ALONG THE MISSISSIPPI
by Gary Scholl and Netha Bell . . . . paperback $9.95

(Continued on Next Page)

(161)

MISSISSIPPI RIVER PO' FOLK
by Pat Wallace . . . . paperback $9.95

STRANGE FOLKS ALONG THE MISSISSIPPI
by Pat Wallace . . . . paperback $9.95

THE VANISHING OUTHOUSE OF IOWA
by Bruce Carlson . . . . paperback $9.95

THE VANISHING OUTHOUSE OF ILLINOIS
by Bruce Carlson . . . . paperback $9.95

THE VANISHING OUTHOUSE OF MINNESOTA
by Bruce Carlson . . . . paperback $9.95

THE VANISHING OUTHOUSE OF WISCONSIN
by Bruce Carlson . . . . paperback $9.95

MISSISSIPPI RIVER COOKIN' BOOK
by Bruce Carlson . . . . paperback $11.95

IOWA'S ROAD KILL COOKBOOK
by Bruce Carlson . . . . paperback $7.95

HITCH HIKING THE UPPER MIDWEST
by Bruce Carlson . . . . paperback $7.95

IOWA, THE LAND BETWEEN THE VOWELS
by Bruce Carlson . . . . paperback $9.95
(Farm Boy Stories From the Early 1900's)

GHOSTS OF SOUTHWEST MINNESOTA
by Ruth Hein . . . . paperback $9.95

GHOSTS OF THE COAST OF MAINE
by Carole Olivieri Schulte . . . . paperback $9.95

ME 'N WESLEY
by Bruce Carlson . . . . paperback $9.95
(Stories about the homemade toys that farm children made and played with around the turn of the century.)

(162)

SOUTH DAKOTA ROAD KILL COOKBOOK
by Bruce Carlson ....paperback $7.95

GHOSTS OF THE BLACK HILLS
by Tom Welch......................paperback $9.95

Some Pretty Tame, But Kinda Funny Stories About Early DAKOTA LADIES-OF-THE-EVENING
by Bruce Carlson ....paperback $9.95

Some Pretty Tame, But Kinda Funny Stories About Early IOWA LADIES-OF-THE EVENING
by Bruce Carlson ....paperback $9.95

Some Pretty Tame, But Kinda Funny Stories About Early ILLINOIS LADIES-OF-THE-EVENING
by Bruce Carlson ....paperback $9.95

Some Pretty Tame, But Kinda Funny Stories About Early MINNESOTA LADIES-OF-THE-EVENING
by Bruce Carlson ....paperback $9.95

Some Pretty Tame, But Kinda Funny Stories About Early WISCONSIN LADIES-OF-THE-EVENING
by Bruce Carlson ....paperback $9.95

Some Pretty Tame, But Kinda Funny Stories About Early MISSOURI LADIES-OF-THE-EVENING
by Bruce Carlson ....paperback $9.95

THE DAKOTA'S VANISHING OUTHOUSE
Bruce Carlson ....paperback $9.95

ILLINOIS' ROAD KILL COOKBOOK
by Bruce Carlson ....paperback $7.95

OLD IOWA HOUSES, YOUNG LOVES
by Bruce Carlson ....paperback $9.95
(Stores about old houses in Iowa and young loves they have known.)

(163)

TERROR IN THE BLACK HILLS
by Dick Kennedy .... paperback $9.95

IOWA'S EARLY HOME REMEDIES
by 26 students at Wapello Elem. School ... paperback $9.95

GHOSTS OF DOOR COUNTY, WISCONSIN
by Geri Rider .... paperback $9.95

TALES OF HACKETT'S CREEK
(1940's Mississippi River Kids)
by Dan Titus .... paperback $9.95

A FIELD GUIDE TO IOWA'S CRITTERS
by Bruce Carlson .... paperback $7.95

A FIELD GUIDE TO ILLINOIS' CRITTERS
by Bruce Carlson .... paperback $7.95

A FIELD GUIDE TO MISSOURI'S CRITTERS
by Bruce Carlson .... paperback $7.95

MISSOURI'S ROADKILL COOKBOOK
by Bruce Carlson .... paperback $7.95

MINNESOTA'S ROADKILL COOKBOOK
by Bruce Carlson .... paperback $7.95

UNSOLVED MYSTERIES OF THE MISSISSIPPI
by Netha Bell .... paperback $9.95

UNDERGROUND MISSOURI
by Bruce Carlson .... paperback $9.95

UNDERGROUND IOWA
by Bruce Carlson .... paperback $9.95

(164)

Need a Gift?

For

- **Shower** • **Birthday** • **Mother's Day** •
  • **Anniversary** • **Christmas** •

Turn Page For Order Form
(Order Now While Supply Lasts!)

TO ORDER COPIES OF
IOWA'S OLD HOUSES
AND NEW LOVES

Please send me _____ copies of **Iowa's Old Houses and New Loves** at $9.95 each. (Make checks payable to **QUIXOTE PRESS**.)

Name _____

Street _____

City _____ State _____ Zip Code ____

SEND ORDERS TO:

QUIXOTE PRESS
R.R. #4, Box 33B
Blvd. Station
Sioux City, Iowa 51109

TO ORDER COPIES OF
IOWA'S OLD HOUSES
AND NEW LOVES

Please send me _____ copies of **Iowa's Old Houses and New Loves** at $9.95 each. (Make checks payable to **QUIXOTE PRESS**.)

Name _____

Street _____

City _____ State _____ Zip Code ____

SEND ORDERS TO:

QUIXOTE PRESS
R.R. #4, Box 33B
Blvd. Station
Sioux City, Iowa 51109

(166)

INDEX

A

B

C

D

E

F

G

H

I

J

K

(Year - Continued)